SUPER SIMPLE

VALENTINE'S DAY

ACTIVITIES

♥ FUN AND EASY HOLIDAY PROJECTS FOR KIDS ♥

Megan Borgert-Spaniol

Consulting Editor, Diane Craig, M.A./Reading Specialist

Super Sandcastle

An Imprint of Abdo Publishing
abdopublishing.com

abdopublishing.com

Published by Abdo Publishing, a division of ABDO, PO Box 398166, Minneapolis, Minnesota 55439.
Copyright © 2018 by Abdo Consulting Group, Inc. International copyrights reserved in all countries.
No part of this book may be reproduced in any form without written permission from the publisher.
Super SandCastle™ is a trademark and logo of Abdo Publishing.

Printed in the United States of America, North Mankato, Minnesota

102017
012018

THIS BOOK CONTAINS RECYCLED MATERIALS

Design: Alison Stuerman, Mighty Media, Inc.
Production: Mighty Media, Inc.
Editor: Rebecca Felix
Cover Photographs: Mighty Media, Inc.; Shutterstock
Interior Photographs: iStockphoto; Mighty Media, Inc.; Shutterstock; Wikimedia Commons

The following manufacturers/names appearing in this book are trademarks:
Con-Tact Brand®, Craft Smart®, Duncan Hines Wilderness®, Elmer's® Glue-All™, Essential
Everyday™, Gold Medal®, Land O Lakes®, Sharpie®

Publisher's Cataloging-in-Publication Data
Names: Borgert-Spaniol, Megan, author.
Title: Super simple Valentine's Day activities: fun and easy holiday projects for kids /
by Megan Borgert-Spaniol.
Other titles: Fun and easy holiday projects for kids
Description: Minneapolis, Minnesota : Abdo Publishing, 2018. | Series: Super simple holidays |
Identifiers: LCCN 2017946528 | ISBN 9781532112485 (lib.bdg.) | ISBN 9781614799900 (ebook)
Subjects: LCSH: Valentine decorations--Juvenile literature. | Handicraft--Juvenile literature. |
    Holiday decorations--Juvenile literature.
Classification: DDC 745.5941618--dc23
LC record available at https://lccn.loc.gov/2017946528

TO ADULT HELPERS

The craft projects in this series are fun and simple. There are just a few things to remember to keep kids safe. Some projects require the use of sharp or hot objects. Also, kids may be using messy materials such as glue or paint. Make sure they protect their clothes and work surfaces. Review the projects before starting and be ready to assist when necessary.

KEY SYMBOLS

Watch for these warning symbols in this book. Here is what each one means.

HOT!
This project requires the use of a stove or oven. Get help!

SHARP!
You will be working with a sharp object. Get help!

CONTENTS 💜🌀

HAPPY HOLIDAYS!

Holidays are great times to celebrate with family and friends. Many people have favorite holiday **traditions**. Some traditions are hundreds of years old. But people start new traditions too, such as making holiday foods and crafts.

VALENTINE'S DAY

Valentine's Day is on February 14. It is a celebration of love. But the holiday did not begin this way. Some people disagree about its **origins**. But many say it began to honor Saint Valentine. He lived in the 200s.

Legends tell of Valentine's **romantic** actions when he was alive. These actions made people think of love. In the 1300s, Valentine's Day became a day to celebrate these feelings.

CELEBRATE VALENTINE'S DAY

Several Valentine's Day **traditions** are common throughout many cultures. How do you celebrate Valentine's Day?

HEARTS

The heart shape has been used as a **symbol** of love for hundreds of years. Because Valentine's Day celebrates love, many people give one another heart-shaped gifts on this holiday. This includes heart-shaped chocolates, cards, jewelry, and more!

FLOWERS

People have used flowers to send messages for hundreds of years. Different flowers represent hope, friendship, and more. Many people give red roses to their sweethearts on February 14. These represent love.

CARDS & POEMS

Sending written Valentine's Day messages dates back to 1415. French royal Charles, Duke of Orléans, wrote a poem for his wife that year. In the 1840s, Esther A. Howland made and sold Valentine's Day cards in the United States. Today, people around the world send their loved ones cards and poems on this holiday.

MATERIALS

Here are some of the materials that you will need for the projects in this book.

BAKING SHEET

BUTTONS

CARD STOCK

CARDBOARD

CELERY

CHERRY PIE FILLING

CHOCOLATE CANDIES

COLORED PAPER

CONTACT PAPER

CRAFT GLUE

CRAFT KNIFE

FLOUR

GLITTER

GOOGLY EYES

HEART-SHAPED
COOKIE CUTTERS

HEAVY WHIPPING
CREAM

HOLE PUNCH

JEWELS

MARKERS

PAINT

PAINTBRUSHES

PARCHMENT
PAPER

PASTRY BRUSH

PENCIL

PHOTO FRAME

PREMADE
PIE DOUGH

RIBBON

ROLLING PIN

SCISSORS

YARN

HEART WREATH

Hang a homemade wreath bursting with love!

WHAT YOU NEED

cardboard

pencil

plate

bowl, smaller than the plate

craft knife

card stock

scissors

colored paper

craft glue

ribbon

tape

10

1 Trace the plate on the cardboard. Trace the bowl within this circle.

2 Have an adult help you use the craft knife to cut out the cardboard ring.

3 Draw a heart on card stock. Cut out the heart. This is the **template**.

4 Trace the template on colored paper to make more hearts. Cut out the hearts.

5 Glue the hearts around the ring. Place each heart so its point faces inward.

6 Repeat steps 3 through 5 to make smaller hearts and add them to the wreath. Glue the small hearts so they **overlap** the large hearts. Make sure all points face inward.

7 Cut a piece of ribbon. Tape its ends to the back of the wreath to make a hanger.

8 Hang your wreath to spread holiday spirit!

CHERRY PIE VALENTINE

Make this tasty treat for someone sweet!

WHAT YOU NEED

flour

premade pie dough

rolling pin

large heart-shaped
   cookie cutter

dinner knife or
   pastry cutter

baking sheet

parchment paper

cherry pie filling

measuring cup

spoon

water

fork

heavy whipping
   cream

pastry brush

white sanding sugar

1 Preheat the oven to 350 **degrees** Fahrenheit. Sprinkle flour over your work surface. Unroll the pie **dough**. Smooth it out with the rolling pin if needed.

2 Cut out two hearts with the cookie cutter. Remove the extra pie dough.

3 Use the knife or pastry cutter to cut a small heart in the center of one large heart. Remove the small heart.

4 Line a baking sheet with parchment paper. Place the large heart without the cutout on the sheet.

5 Spoon ½ cup of cherry filling onto the heart that is on the baking sheet.

(continued on next page)

6 Spread the filling over the heart. Leave a small border of **dough** around the heart's edges.

7 Use your finger to dab water around the edge of the dough.

8 Place the heart with the cutout on top of the heart with the filling.

9 Use a fork to **crimp** both hearts' edges together.

10 Lightly brush the pie **dough** with heavy whipping cream.

11 Sprinkle white sanding sugar over the whipping cream.

12 Bake the pie for 15 to 20 minutes or until golden.

13 Serve this holiday treat to a friend or family member!

TIP Make another heart pie with a different fruit filling. Try blueberry or apple!

CANDY TIC-TAC-TOE

Chocolate game pieces make this Valentine's Day game super sweet!

WHAT YOU NEED

card stock

pencil

scissors

craft glue

ribbon

ruler

decorative materials, such as glitter, jewels & stickers

chocolate candies

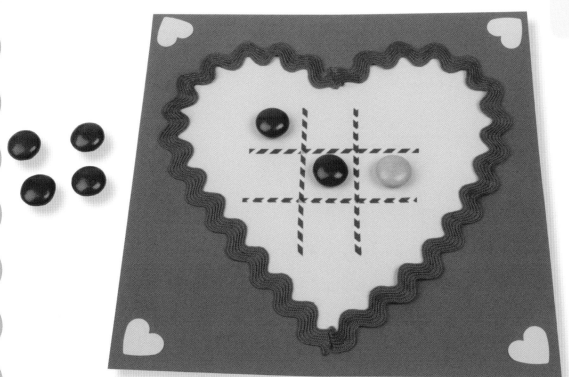

16

1 Draw a large heart on card stock. Cut out the shape.

2 Cut a sheet of different-colored card stock into a square. Glue the heart onto it.

3 Cut four pieces of ribbon. Make them each 2¼ inches (6 cm) long.

4 Glue two ribbons **horizontally** across the heart. Space them ¾ inch (2 cm) apart. Glue the other two ribbons vertically across the first ribbons. Space them ¾ inch (2 cm) apart.

5 Decorate the game board if you like! Use markers, glitter, jewels, or stickers.

6 Repeat steps 1 through 5 to make several game cards.

7 Give your tic-tac-toe cards to friends for Valentine's Day! Include chocolate candies to use as game pieces.

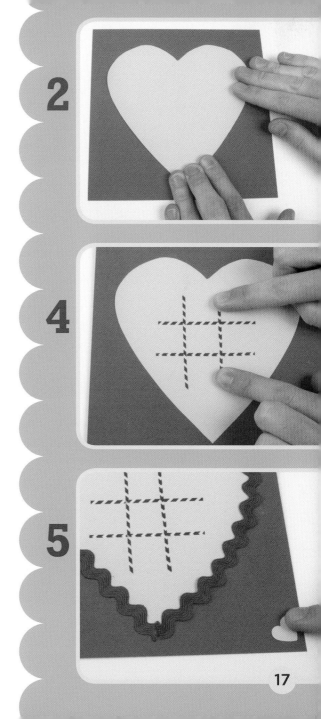

17

BUTTON HEART ART

Craft fun color combinations with this framed work of heart!

WHAT YOU NEED

photo frame

card stock

pencil

scissors

buttons of various shapes, sizes & colors

craft glue

1 Use the cardboard backing from the frame to trace a rectangle on card stock. Cut out the rectangle.

2 Lightly draw a heart inside the rectangle.

3 Arrange buttons so they completely fill in the heart.

4 Glue the buttons to the card stock. Let the glue dry.

5 Remove the frame's glass. Secure the card stock inside the frame.

6 Decorate the outside of the frame by gluing on a few buttons.

7 Give your heart art to someone you love!

TIP Erase the pencil outline as you glue on the buttons. This way, it won't show in your final art.

SWEETHEART FISH

Turn hearts into friendly little fish!

WHAT YOU NEED
pencil
card stock
scissors
craft glue
googly eyes

1 Draw hearts of various sizes on colored sheets of card stock. Cut out the shapes.

2 Arrange the hearts to look like a **tropical** fish. Glue the hearts together.

3 Glue one googly eye to the fish's head.

4 Repeat steps 1 through 3 to make more fish. Try different color combinations and arrangements.

5 Cut a wavy pattern at the top of a blue sheet of card stock. Glue your fish to the card stock.

6 Put your sweet school of fish on display! What other animals can you create using hearts?

TIP Use larger hearts for heads and bodies. Smaller hearts can be used for fins and tails.

CELERY STAMP BOUQUET

Use celery to create a sweet holiday bouquet of flowers!

WHAT YOU NEED

stalk of celery

sharp knife

cutting board

red, pink & green paint

paper plates

card stock

paper towels

paintbrush

1 Have an adult help you cut the celery stalk so its ends are even.

2 Pour a little red and pink paint on two separate paper plates.

3 Dip the cut end of the celery in pink paint.

4 Stamp the celery onto the card stock. The pattern should look like flowers!

5 Rinse the paint from the celery stalk. Dry the cut ends. Then repeat steps 3 and 4 using the red paint.

6 Paint green stems and leaves on your flowers.

7 Present your stamped **bouquet** to someone special!

YARN
HEART ORNAMENTS

Turn yarn into hearts that you can hang anywhere!

WHAT YOU NEED

cardboard

marker

scissors

craft knife

cutting mat

yarn

ruler

1 Draw a heart on the cardboard. Draw a smaller heart inside of it.

2 Cut out the large heart. Have an adult help you cut out the smaller heart with a craft knife.

3 Tie a long piece of yarn around the top of the heart frame.

4 Wrap the yarn **snugly** around the frame. Keep wrapping until the yarn covers the entire frame. If you run out of yarn, tie on a new piece and continue wrapping.

5 When you reach the top of the heart, tie the yarn around the frame. Cut the yarn 8 inches (20 cm) from the heart. Tie the end of the yarn around the top of the heart to make a hanger.

6 Make more heart ornaments. Then hang them to celebrate Valentine's Day!

LOVE BUG CARD

Send a lovely greeting with this little bug!

WHAT YOU NEED

card stock

marker or pencil

scissors

craft glue

googly eyes

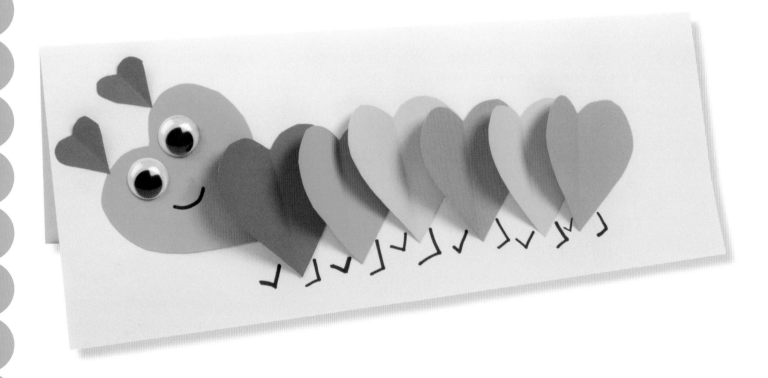

1 Draw a small heart on card stock. Cut out the shape.

2 Trace the heart on five different colors of card stock. Cut out the hearts. These will form the bug's body.

3 Cut out a heart that is slightly bigger. This will become the bug's head.

4 Cut out two smaller hearts. These will be used for the bug's antennae.

5 Fold all of the hearts in half down their centers. Open them back up.

6 Fold a sheet of card stock in half **lengthwise** to make a card.

7 Glue the bug's head onto the front of the card near one side.

(continued on next page)

27

9

10

11

8 Glue one body heart next to the head. Glue down the right half of the heart. Let the left half **overlap** the bottom corner of the head.

9 Glue down the right half of another body heart next to the first heart. Let the left half of the new heart overlap the first heart.

10 Repeat step 9 with the remaining body hearts.

11 Glue down one half of each antennae heart above the head. Glue googly eyes onto the head.

12 Draw legs and a mouth.

13 Give your little love bug to a loved one!

HEART SUNCATCHER

Watch sunlight stream through a colorful suncatcher!

(continued on next page)

WHAT YOU NEED
card stock
marker or pencil
scissors
tissue paper
contact paper
hole punch
ribbon

1 Draw a large heart on the card stock. Draw a smaller heart within the large heart. Cut the hearts out to create a frame.

2 Cut different colors of tissue paper into small squares.

3 Cut a square piece of contact paper slightly larger than the heart. Peel the backing paper off. Place the heart frame on the sticky side of the contact paper.

4 Fill in the heart frame with the tissue paper squares. Let the squares **overlap** one another.

5 Cut another piece of contact paper. Carefully lay its sticky side on top of the heart. Press it smooth.

6 Cut out the heart. Leave a small border of sealed contact paper around it.

7 Punch a hole at the top of the heart.

8 Tie a piece of ribbon through the hole to make a hanger.

9 Hang your suncatcher in a window. Watch its colors glow as sunlight shines through!

GLOSSARY

bouquet – a bunch of flowers or plants gathered together or arranged in a vase.

crimp – to pinch or press something to make it bent or wavy.

dough – a thick mixture of flour, water, and other ingredients used in baking.

horizontal – in the same direction as, or parallel to, the ground.

legend – a story passed down through history that may not be true.

lengthwise – in the direction of the longest side.

origin – where something starts, or the cause of something.

overlap – to lie partly on top of something.

romantic – of or having to do with love.

snugly – in a tight or close-fitting way.

symbol – an object or picture that stands for or represents something.

template – a shape or pattern that is drawn or cut around to make the same shape in another material.

tradition – a belief or practice passed through a family or group of people.

tropical – like or related to the hottest areas on Earth.